# THE FAMILY TREASURY

## of

# CLASSIC CHRISTMAS CAROLS

# THE FAMILY TREASURY of CLASSIC CHRISTMAS CAROLS

ILLUSTRATED BY SARAH GIBB

COURAGE BOOKS

AN IMPRINT OF RUNNING PRESS
PHILADELPHIA • LONDON

9   8   7   6   5   4
Digit on the right indicates the number of this printing

Library of Congress Cataloging-in-Publication Number 2002100687

ISBN 0-7624-1392-1

Cover and interior design by Bill Jones
Edited by Sara Phillips
Typography: Berkeley

This book may be ordered by mail from the publisher.
*But try your bookstore first!*

Published by Courage Books, an imprint of
Running Press Book Publishers
125 South Twenty-second Street
Philadelphia, Pennsylvania 19103-4399

Visit us on the web!
www.runningpress.com

# CONTENTS

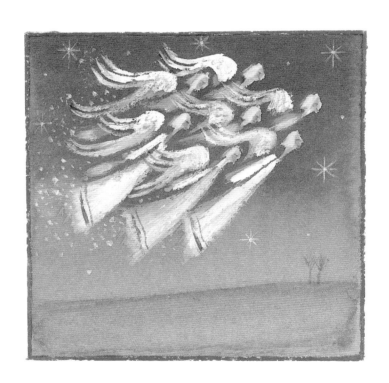

The stamp of snowy shoes outside, a muffled giggle, silence, and then, a chorus of voices in the chill air, singing songs of the season. Caroling has a place at the heart of our holiday celebrations.

The tradition of caroling dates back five hundred years to the English "waits," groups of minstrels given the privilege of walking the town at Christmastime, singing at houses and receiving gifts from the townspeople. More recently, caroling was taken up by groups of boys, often unskilled in singing, but demanding a tip nonetheless! Caroling as we know it today began in Victorian times and continues little changed.

Through the years, songs other than carols have been sung at Christmastime. Some of the songs we call carols are hymns or popular songs that celebrate the holiday season. Others are traditional tunes sung with more contemporary lyrics.

The songs sung by carolers have changed as much as caroling itself, but the joy of singing together at Christmastime remains as great as ever!

# Angels We Have

### 1
Angels we have heard on high,
Sweetly singing o'er the plains;
And the mountains, in reply,
Echoing their joyous strains:

*Chorus:*
Gloria in excelsis Deo,
Gloria in excelsis Deo!

### 2
Shepherds, why this jubilee?
Why your joyful strains prolong?
What the gladsome tidings be
That inspire your heav'nly song?

# Heard on High

### 3

Come to Bethlehem and see
Him whose birth the angels sing.
Come adore on bended knee
Christ the Lord, our newborn King.

### 4

See Him in a manger laid,
Whom the choirs of angels praise.
Mary, Joseph, lend your aid
While our hearts in love we raise.

*Repeat Chorus*

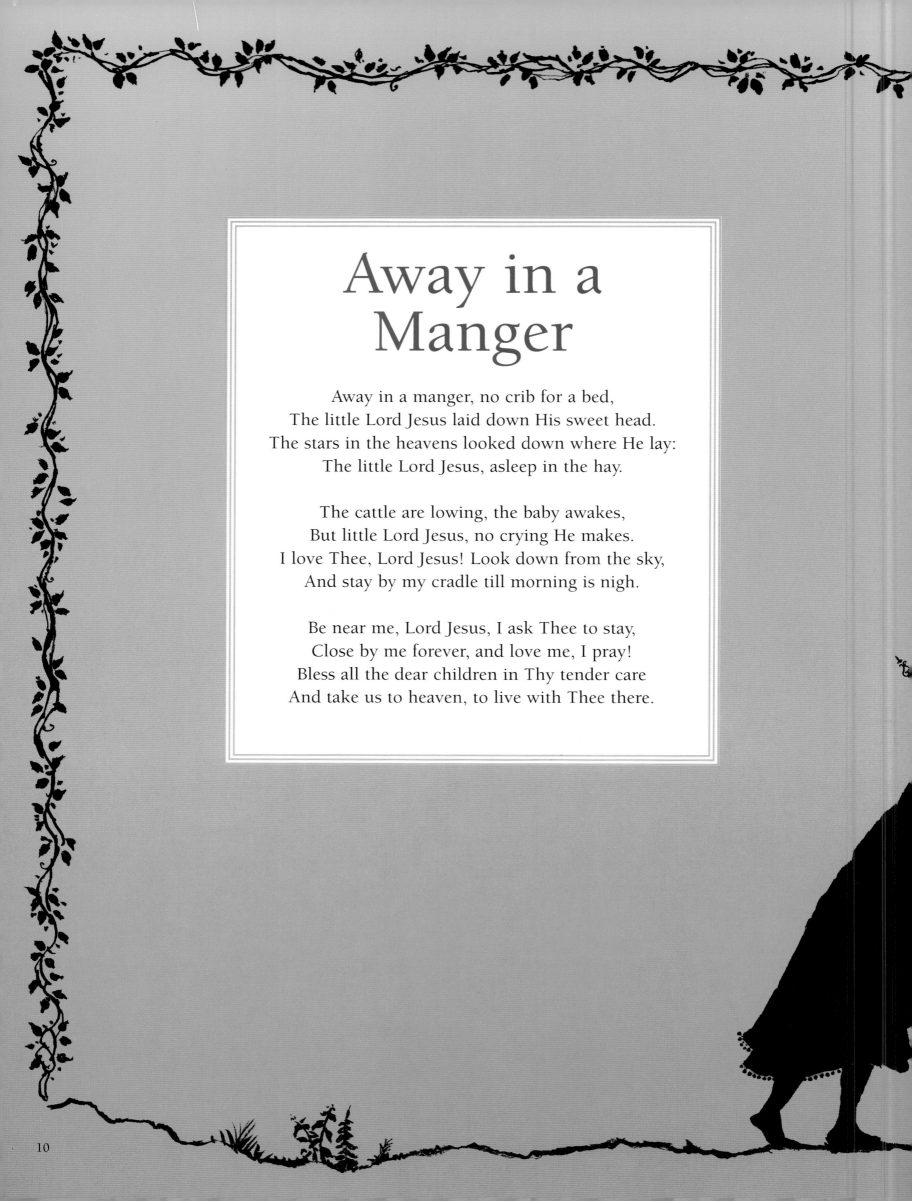

# Away in a Manger

Away in a manger, no crib for a bed,
The little Lord Jesus laid down His sweet head.
The stars in the heavens looked down where He lay:
The little Lord Jesus, asleep in the hay.

The cattle are lowing, the baby awakes,
But little Lord Jesus, no crying He makes.
I love Thee, Lord Jesus! Look down from the sky,
And stay by my cradle till morning is nigh.

Be near me, Lord Jesus, I ask Thee to stay,
Close by me forever, and love me, I pray!
Bless all the dear children in Thy tender care
And take us to heaven, to live with Thee there.

# Deck the Halls

Deck the halls with boughs of holly,
Fa la la la la, la la la la.
'Tis the season to be jolly,
Fa la la la la, la la la la.
Don we now our gay apparel,
Fa la la, la la la, la la la.
Troll the ancient Yuletide carol:
Fa la la la la, la la la la.

See the blazing Yule before us,
Fa la la la la, la la la la.
Strike the harp and join the chorus,
Fa la la la la, la la la la.
Follow me in merry measure,
Fa la la, la la la, la la la,
While I tell of Yuletide treasure,
Fa la la la la, la la la la.

Fast away the old year passes,
Fa la la la la, la la la la.
Hail the new, ye lads and lasses,
Fa la la la la, la la la la.
Sing we joyous, all together,
Fa la la, la la la, la la la,
Heedless of the wind and weather,
Fa la la la la, la la la la.

# The First Noel

### 1

The First Noel, the angels did say
Was to certain poor shepherds in fields as they lay,
In fields where they lay, keeping their sheep,
On a cold winter's night that was so deep.

### *Chorus*:

Noel, Noel, Noel, Noel,
Born is the King of Israel!

### 2

They lookèd up and saw a star,
Shining in the East, but beyond them far.
And unto the Earth it gave a great light,
And so it continued, both day and night.

### 3

And by the light of that same star
Three Wise Men came from country far.
To seek for a King was their intent,
And to follow the star wherever it went.

### 4

This star drew nigh to the northwest.
Over Bethlehem it took its rest,
And there it did both stop and stay
Right over the stable where Jesus lay.

## 5

Then they did know and in wonder confide
That within that house a King did reside.
One entered in then, with his own eyes to see
And discovered the Babe in poverty.

## 6

Between the stalls of the oxen, forlorn,
This Child on that cold night in truth was born.
And for want of a crib, Mary did Him lay
In the depths of a manger amongst the hay.

## 7

Then entered in all those Wise Men three,
Fell reverently upon bended knee,
And offered there, in His presence,
Gifts of gold and of myrrh and of frankincense.

*Repeat Chorus*

# God Rest Ye M[e

### 1

God rest ye merry, gentlemen;
Let nothing you dismay.
Remember, Christ our Savior
Was born on Christmas Day,
To save us all from Satan's pow'r
When we had gone astray.

### *Chorus:*

Oh, tidings of comfort and joy,
Comfort and joy,
Oh, tidings of comfort and joy!

### 2

'Twas in the town of Bethlehem
This blessed Babe was born.
They laid Him in a manger
Where oxen feed on corn,
And Mary knelt and prayed to God
Upon that blessed morn.

### 3

From God our Heav'nly Father
A host of angels came
Unto some certain shepherds
With tidings of the same:
That there was born in Bethlehem
The Son of God by name.

### 4

"Fear not," then said the angels,
"Let nothing you affright.
This day is born a Savior
Of virtue, pow'r, and might,
To ransom you from Sin and Death
And vanquish Satan quite."

# rry, Gentlemen

### 5

The shepherds, at these tidings,
Rejoicèd much in mind,
And on that windy plain they left
Their sleeping flocks behind,
And straight they went to Bethlehem,
Their newborn King to find.

### 6

Now when they came to Bethlehem,
Where our sweet Savior lay,
They found Him in a manger,
Where oxen feed on hay.
His blessed Mother, kneeling down,
Unto the Lord did pray.

### 7

With sudden joy and gladness
The shepherds were beguiled,
To see the King of Israel
And Holy Mary mild.
With them, in cheerfulness and love
Rejoice each mother's child!

### 8

Now to the Lord sing praises,
All you within this place,
And in true loving brotherhood
Each other now embrace,
For Christmas doth in all inspire
A glad and cheerful face.

*Repeat Chorus*

# Good King Wenceslas

Good King Wenceslas looked out
On the Feast of Stephen,
When the snow lay 'round about,
Deep and crisp and even.
Brightly shone the moon that night,
Though the frost was cruel,
When a poor man came in sight,
Gath'ring winter fuel.

"Hither, page, and stand by me!
If thou has heard telling,
Yonder peasant, who is he?
Where and what his dwelling?"
"Sire, he lives a good league hence,
Underneath the mountain,
Right against the forest fence
By Saint Agnes' fountain."

"Bring me flesh and bring me wine!
Bring me pine-logs hither!
Thou and I will see him dine
When we bear them thither."
Page and monarch, forth they went;
Forth they went together,
Through the rude wind's wild lament
And the bitter weather.

"Sire, the night grows darker now,
And the wind blows stronger.
Fails my heart, I know not how
I can go much longer!"
"Mark my footsteps, my good page.
Tread thou in them boldly.
Thou shall feel this winter's rage
Freeze thy blood less coldly."

In his master's steps he trod,
Where the snow lay dinted.
Heat was in the very sod
Which the Saint had printed.
Therefore, Christian men, be sure,
Wealth or rank possessing,
Ye who now will bless the poor
Shall yourselves find blessing.

# Hark! The Hera

## 1

Hark! The herald angels sing,
"Glory to the newborn King!
Peace on Earth and mercy mild,
God and sinners reconciled."
Joyful all ye nations, rise!
Join the triumphs of the skies.
With th'angelic host proclaim,
"Christ is born in Bethlehem!"

*Chorus:*
Hark! The herald angels sing,
"Glory to the newborn King!"

# d Angels Sing

### 2
Christ, by highest Heav'n adored,
Christ, the everlasting Lord,
Late in time, behold Him come,
Offspring of the Virgin's womb.
Veiled in flesh the Godhead see.
Hail in th'Incarnate Deity
Pleased as Man with men to dwell–
Jesus, our Emmanuel!

### 3
Mild He lays His glory by,
Born that man no more may die,
Born to raise the sons of Earth,
Born to give them second birth.
Light and life to all He brings,
Ris'n with healing in His wings.
Hail, the Sun of Righteousness!
Hail, the Heav'n-born Prince of Peace!

*Repeat Chorus*

# The Holly and the Ivy

### 1
The holly and the ivy
Now both are well grown,
Of all the trees that are in the wood
The holly bears the crown.

### *Chorus:*
The rising of the sun,
The running of the deer,
The playing of the merry organ,
The singing in the choir.

### 2
The holly bears a blossom
As white as the lily flower,
And Mary bore sweet Jesus Christ
To be our sweet Savior.

### 3
The holly bears a berry
As red as any blood,
And Mary bore sweet Jesus Christ
To do poor sinners good.

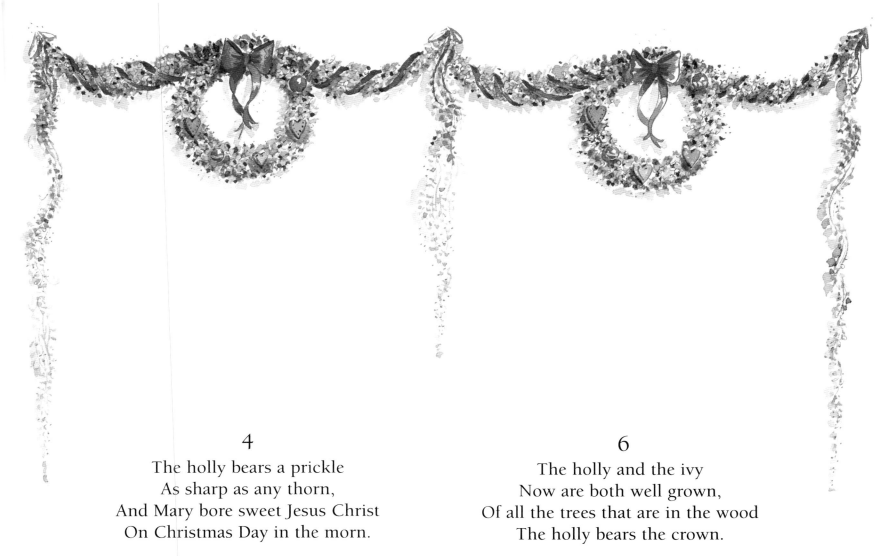

**4**

The holly bears a prickle
As sharp as any thorn,
And Mary bore sweet Jesus Christ
On Christmas Day in the morn.

**5**

The holly bears a bark
As bitter as any gall,
And Mary bore sweet Jesus Christ
For to redeem us all.

**6**

The holly and the ivy
Now are both well grown,
Of all the trees that are in the wood
The holly bears the crown.

*Repeat Chorus*

# It Came Upon a Midnight Clear

It came upon a midnight clear,
That glorious song of old,
From angels bending near the Earth
To touch their harps of gold:
"Peace on the earth!
Good will to men,
From Heaven's all-gracious King!"
The world in solemn stillness lay
To hear the angels sing.

Still through the cloven skies they come,
With seraphs' wings unfurled;
And still their heavenly music floats
O'er all the weary world.
Above its sad and lowly plains
They bend on hovering wing.
And ever o'er its Babel sounds
The blessed angels sing.

Yet with the woes of sin and strife,
The world has suffered long.
Beneath the angels' strains have rolled
Two thousand years of wrong;
And man, at war with man, hears not
The love-song which they bring.
Oh, hush the noise, ye men of strife,
And hear the angels sing!

And ye, beneath life's crushing load,
Whose shoulders are bending low,
Who toil along the climbing way
With painful steps, and slow,
Take heart! For comfort, hope, and joy
Come swiftly on the wing.
Oh, rest beside the weary road
And hear the angels sing!

For lo! The days are hast'ning on,
As prophets knew of old,
And with the ever-circling years
Comes 'round the time foretold,
When love shall reign, and men declare
The Prince of Peace their King;
And all the Earth send back the song
Which now the angels sing.

# Jingle Bells

**1**

Dashing through the snow
In a one-horse open sleigh,
O'er the fields we go,
Laughing all the way.
Bells on bobtail ring,
Making spirits bright.
What fun it is to laugh and sing
A sleighing song tonight!

*Chorus:*
Jingle bells! Jingle bells!
Jingle all the way!
Oh, what fun it is to ride
In a one-horse open sleigh, hey!
Jingle bells! Jingle bells!
Jingle all the way!
Oh, what fun it is to ride
In a one-horse open sleigh!

**2**

A day or two ago, I thought I'd take a ride,
And soon Miss Fannie Bright
Was seated by my side.
The horse was lean and lank,
But hardly worth his hay.
He veered into a drifted bank
And overturned the sleigh!

### 3

Now the ground is white.
Go for it while you're young.
Take the girls tonight
And sing this sleighing song.
Just rent a bobtail'd bay,
Two-forty for his speed.
Then hitch him to an open sleigh,
And crack! You'll take the lead!

### 4

You won't mind the cold,
The robe is thick and warm.
Snow falls on the road,
Silv'ring every form,
The woods are dark and still.
The horse is trotting fast.
He'll pull the sleigh around the hill
And home again at last.

*Repeat Chorus*

# Jolly Old
# Saint Nicholas

Jolly old Saint Nicholas,
Lean your ear this way.
Don't you tell a single soul
What I'm going to say.
Christmas Eve is coming soon!
Now, you dear old man,
Whisper what you'll bring to me.
Tell me, if you can.

When the clock is striking twelve,
When I'm fast asleep,
Down the chimney broad and black
With your pack you'll creep.
All the stockings you will find,
Hanging in a row.
Mine will be the shortest one,
You'll be sure to know.

Johnny wants a pair of skates.
Mary wants a sled.
Susie wants a picture book,
One she's never read.
Now I think I'll leave to you
What to give the rest.
Choose for me, dear Santa Claus,
You will know the best.

# Joy to the World

Joy to the world!
The Lord is come.
Let Earth receive her King.
Let ev'ry heart prepare Him room,
And Heav'n and Nature sing,
And Heav'n and Nature sing,
And Heav'n, and Heav'n and Nature sing.

Joy to the World!
The Savior reigns;
Let men their songs employ,
While fields and floods, rocks, hills, and plains,
Repeat the sounding joy,
Repeat the sounding joy,
Repeat, repeat the sounding joy.

No more let sins
And sorrows grow,
Nor thorns infest the ground;
He comes to make His blessings flow
Far as the curse is found,
Far as the curse is found,
Far as, far as the curse is found.

He rules the world with Truth and Grace,
And makes the nations prove
The glories of His righteousness,
And wonders of His love,
And wonders of His love,
And wonders, wonders of His love.

# Oh Christmas Tree

Oh Christmas Tree,
Oh Christmas Tree,
With lush green boughs unchanging–
Green when the summer is bright,
And when the forest's cold and white.
Oh Christmas Tree,
Oh Christmas Tree,
With lush green boughs unchanging!

Oh Christmas Tree,
Oh Christmas Tree,
Here once again to awe us,
You bear round fruits of Christmas past,
Spun out of silver, gold, and glass.
Oh Christmas Tree,
Oh Christmas Tree,
Here once again to awe us!

Oh Christmas Tree,
Oh Christmas Tree,
We gladly bid you welcome.
A pyramid of light you seem,
A galaxy of stars that gleam.
Oh Christmas Tree,
Oh Christmas Tree,
We gladly bid you welcome.

Oh Christmas Tree,
Oh Christmas Tree,
You fill the air with fragrance.
You shrink to very tiny size,
Reflected in the children's eyes.
Oh Christmas Tree,
Oh Christmas Tree,
You fill the air with fragrance.

Oh Christmas Tree,
Oh Christmas Tree,
What presents do you shelter?
Rich wrappings hide the gifts from sight,
Done up in bows and ribbons tight.
Oh Christmas Tree,
Oh Christmas Tree,
What presents do you shelter?

Oh Christmas Tree,
Oh Christmas Tree,
Your green limbs teach a lesson:
That constancy and faithful cheer
Are gifts to cherish all the year.
Oh Christmas Tree,
Oh Christmas Tree,
Your green limbs teach a lesson.

# Oh Come, All Ye Faithful

**1**

Oh come, all ye faithful,
Joyful and triumphant,
Oh come ye, oh come ye to Bethlehem.
Come and behold Him,
Born the King of Angels.

*Chorus:*

Oh come, let us adore Him,
Oh come, let us adore Him,
Oh come, let us adore Him,
Christ the Lord!

**2**

Sing, choirs of angels,
Sing in exultation.
Oh Sing, all ye citizens of Heav'n above:
"Glory to God,
Glory in the highest."

**3**

Oh True God of True God,
Light of Light eternal
Lo! He abhors not the Virgin's womb.
Son of the Father,
Begotten not created.

**4**

See how the shepherds,
Summoned to his cradle,
Leaving their flocks, draw nigh to gaze;
We too will thither
Bend our joyful footsteps.

**5**

Yea, Lord, we greet Thee,
Born this happy morning.
Jesus, to Thee all glory be giv'n,
Word of the Father,
Now in flesh appearing.

*Repeat Chorus*

# Oh Little Town
# of Bethlehem

Oh little town of Bethlehem, how still we see thee lie!
Above thy deep and dreamless sleep the silent starts go by.
Yet in thy dark streets shineth the everlasting light:
The hopes and fears of all the years are met in thee tonight.

For Christ is born of Mary, and gathered all above,
While mortals sleep, the angels keep their watch of wond'ring love.
Oh, morning stars together, proclaim the holy birth,
And praises sing to God the King, and peace to men on Earth.

How silently, how silently the wondrous gift is given!
So God imparts to human hearts the blessings of His heaven.
No ear may hear His coming; but in this world of sin,
Where meek souls will recieve Him still, the dear Christ enters in.

O holy Child of Bethlehem, descend to us, we pray;
Cast out our sin and enter in—be born in us today.
We hear the Christmas angels the great glad tidings tell–
Oh, come to us, abide with us, Our Lord Immanuel!

# Silent Night

Silent night, holy night!
All is calm, all is bright
'Round yon Virgin Mother and Child—
Holy infant, so tender and mild.
Sleep in heavenly peace,
Sleep in heavenly peace.

Silent night, holy night!
Shepherds quake at the sight.
Glories stream from Heaven afar,
Heav'nly hosts sing, "Alleluia,
Christ the Savior is born,
Christ the Savior is born!"

Silent night, holy night!
Son of God, love's pure light,
Radiance beams from Thy holy face,
With the dawn of redeeming grace.
Jesus, Lord at Thy birth,
Jesus, Lord at Thy birth!

# The Twelve Days of Christmas

On the first day of Christmas,
My true love gave to me
A partridge in a pear tree.

On the second day of Christmas,
My true love gave to me
Two turtle doves,
And a partridge in a pear tree.

On the third day of Christmas,
My true love gave to me
Three French hens,
Two turtle doves,
And a partridge in a pear tree.

On the fourth day of Christmas,
My true love gave to me
Four calling birds…

On the fifth day of Christmas,
My true love gave to me,
five golden rings...

On the sixth day of Christmas,
My true love gave to me
Six geese a laying…

On the seventh day of Christmas,
My true love gave to me
Seven swans a-swimming…

On the eighth day of Christmas,
My true love gave to me
Eight maids a-milking…

On the ninth day of Christmas,
My true love gave to me
Nine ladies dancing…

gold rings...

On the tenth day of Christmas,
My true love gave to me
Ten lords a-leaping…

On the eleventh day of Christmas,
My true love gave to me
Eleven pipers piping…

On the twelfth day of Christmas,
My true love gave to me
Twelve drummers drumming,
Eleven pipers piping,
Ten lords a-leaping,
Nine ladies dancing,
Eight maids a-milking,
Seven swans a-swimming,
Six geese a-laying,
Five golden rings,
Four calling birds,
Three French hens,
Two turtle doves,
And a partridge in a pear tree.

# Up on the Rooftop

### 1

Up on the rooftop, reindeer pause.
Out jumps good old Santa Claus!
Down through the chimney, with lots of toys—
All for the little ones' Christmas joys.

### Chorus:

Ho, ho, ho! Who wouldn't go?
Ho, ho, ho! Who wouldn't go
Up on the rooftop—
Click, click, click!—
Down through the chimney
With good St. Nick.

### 2

First comes the stocking of little Nell.
Oh, dear Santa, fill it well!
Give her a dolly that laughs and cries,
One that can open and shut her eyes.

### 3

Next hangs the stocking of brother Will.
It won't take very much to fill—
Give him a hammer and lots of tacks,
Plus a red ball and a whip that cracks.

**4**

Reindeer are restless beside your sleigh,
Eager to leave and be on their way.
But on the mantel, I've left for you
Apples, an orange, and warm milk too.

**5**

Last is a stocking that's deep and strong—
I've been a good boy all year long!
Please, if you have them, and if they'll fit,
Give me a bat and a catcher's mitt.

*Repeat Chorus*

# We Three Kings of Orient Are

### All:
We three kings of Orient are
Bearing gifts, we traverse afar—
Field and fountain,
moor and mountain—
Following yonder star.

### Chorus:
Oh, star of wonder, star of night,
Star of royal beauty bright,
Westward leading, still proceeding,
Guide us to thy perfect light.

### King Melchoir:
Born a king on Bethlehem's plain—
Gold I bring, to crown Him again—
King for ever, ceasing never,
Over us all to reign.

### Chorus

### King Gaspar:
Frankincense to offer have I.
Incense owns a Deity nigh.
Prayer and praising, all men raising,
Worship Him, God most high!

### Chorus

### King Balthazar:
Myrrh is mine: its bitter perfume
Breathes a life of gathering gloom,
Sorrowing, sighing, bleeding, dying,
Sealed in the stone-cold tomb.

### Chorus

### All:
Glorious now, behold Him arise:
King and God and sacrifice!
Heav'n sings, "Ha-le-lu-ia!"
"Ha-ah-le-lu-ia!" the Earth replies.

# We Wish You a Merry Christmas

## 1

We wish you a Merry Christmas,
We wish you a Merry Christmas,
We wish you a Merry Christmas
And a Happy New Year!

*Chorus:*
Glad tidings we bring
To you and your kin.
We wish you a merry Christmas,
And a Happy New Year.

## 2

Oh, bring us some figgy pudding,
Oh, bring us some figgy pudding,
Oh, bring us some figgy pudding
And a glass of good cheer!

## 3

We won't go until we get some,
We won't go until we get some,
We won't go until we get some
So bring it right here!

### 4

We'll sing you some happy carols,
We'll sing you some happy carols,
We'll sing you some happy carols
To ravish your ear!

### 5

We have quite the finest voices,
We have quite the finest voices,
We have quite the finest voices
That you'll ever hear!

### 6

We wish you a Merry Christmas,
We wish you a Merry Christmas,
We wish you a Merry Christmas
And a Happy New Year!

*Chorus:*
Glad tidings we bring
To you and your kin.
We wish you a merry Christmas,
And a Happy New Year.

# What Child Is This?

### 1

What Child is this who, laid to rest,
On Mary's lap is sleeping;
Whom angels greet with anthems sweet,
While shepherds watch are keeping?

### *Chorus:*

This, this is Christ the King,
Whom shepherds guard and angels sing.
Haste, haste to bring Him laud,
The Babe, the Son of Mary.

### 2

Why lies He in such mean estate,
Where ox and ass are feeding?
Good Christian, fear for sinners here,
The silent Word is pleading.

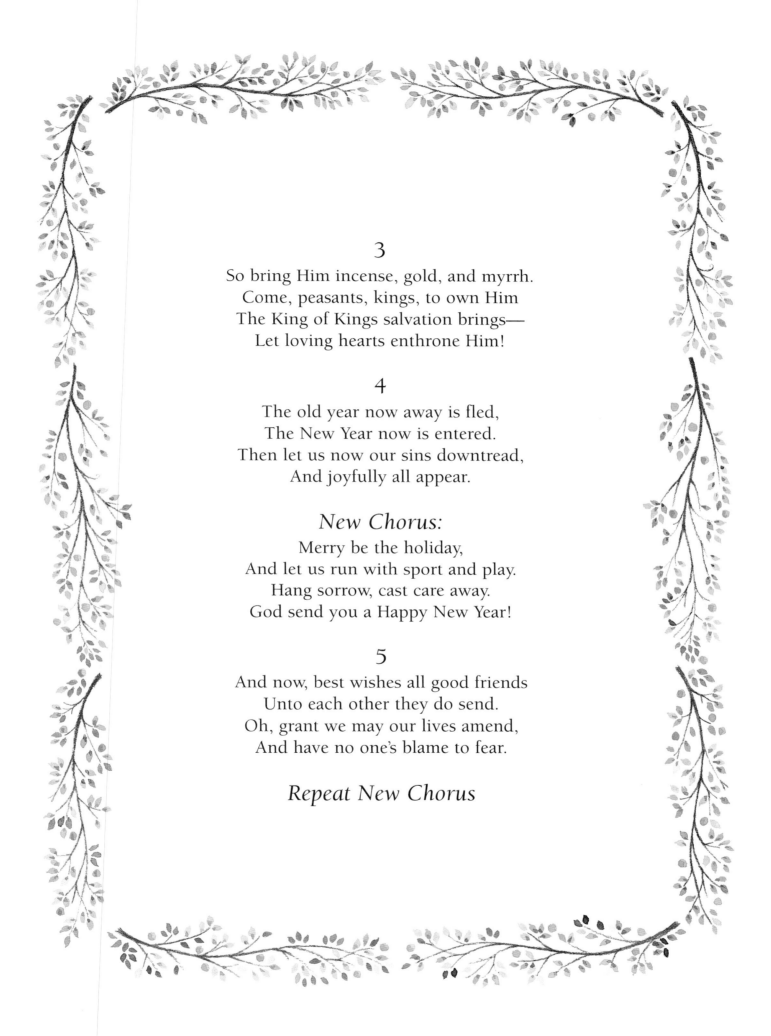

### 3

So bring Him incense, gold, and myrrh.
Come, peasants, kings, to own Him
The King of Kings salvation brings—
Let loving hearts enthrone Him!

### 4

The old year now away is fled,
The New Year now is entered.
Then let us now our sins downtread,
And joyfully all appear.

### *New Chorus:*

Merry be the holiday,
And let us run with sport and play.
Hang sorrow, cast care away.
God send you a Happy New Year!

### 5

And now, best wishes all good friends
Unto each other they do send.
Oh, grant we may our lives amend,
And have no one's blame to fear.

### *Repeat New Chorus*

Merry Christmas

48